A Portrait of the Bride: The Shulamite

Rebecca Park Totilo

A Portrait of the Bride: The Shulamite

Cover Design by Rebecca Park Totilo

Published by Rebecca at the Well Foundation, PO Box 60044, St. Petersburg, Florida 33784.

Scripture references are taken from the King James Version of the Bible.

ISBN 978-0-9749115-1-9

Table of Contents

Introduction

*T*he Song of Solomon is a very well-orchestrated book of prose with multiple scores, layers, and levels of understanding. Some interpret it to be a simple, literal, love affair between a shepherd boy/king and his Shulamite bride. Others describe it as a how-to manual on biblical love-making. It is much more than that. The Song of Solomon is a word of prophecy and the prophet Solomon is acting out a prophetic charade with his bride and the daughters of Jerusalem. This little book, once hidden behind a veil, is now being revealed to those who have ears to hear.

A Portrait of the Bride: The Shulamite will take you through a study of the attributes of the Bride of Christ as described in the Song of Solomon chapter 4:1-7.

Gladdening the Bride

Behold, thou [art] fair, my love; behold, thou [art] fair; thou [hast] doves' eyes within thy locks: thy hair [is] as a flock of goats, that appear from mount Gilead. Thy teeth [are] like a flock [of sheep that are even] shorn, which came up from the washing; whereof every one bear twins, and none [is] barren among them. Thy lips [are] like a thread of scarlet, and thy speech [is] comely: thy temples [are] like a piece of a pomegranate within thy locks. Thy neck [is] like the tower of David built for an armory, whereon there hang a thousand bucklers, all shields of mighty men. Thy two breasts [are] like two young roes that are twins, which feed among the lilies. Until the day break, and the shadows flee away, I will get me to the mountain of myrrh, and to the hill of frankincense. Thou [art] all fair, my love; [there is] no spot in thee.

— Song of Solomon 4:1-7

*I*n Song of Solomon chapter 4, the scene opens with guests gathered around the feast, in the marriage hall. Solomon begins to draw special attention to the Shulamite's physical beauty and characteristics he observes in her.

In Judaism, gladdening the bride with praises of her beauty and splendor on her wedding day was a *Mitzvah* (commandment) and still remains a religious obligation for many Jews to this day. These are examples of the high praises the groom bestows upon his bride and Solomon is no exception.

He uses common imagery of the day to praise her. Not with just meaningless, empty words of flattery as you hear in today's pop music, but with well-chosen thought-out words that carry rich meaning.

The symbols and images Solomon uses to portray the beauty of his Shulamite bride may seem strange to us, as he describes her hair as "a flock of goats, that appear from mount Gilead" (4:1) and her neck as "the tower of David built for an armory, whereon there hang a thousand bucklers" (4:4). Today, one would not consider his remarks as flattery.

However, his compliments reflected the cultural patterns of the ancient world. One author suggests, "To those who lived in Solomon's time, the rippling effect of a flock of goats moving down a hillside was, indeed, a thing of beauty." As we will learn, such use of images and symbols do reflect, in fact, a thing of splendor for those who are part of the Messiah's bride.

Solomon describes eight distinct virtues emerging in her life and is projecting her new image in terms of what she will become. Romans 4:17 says God "calleth those things which be not as though they were," even though it is not what she presently manifests. She is, in reality, a mirror-image of him (the bridegroom), reflecting his character.

On several occasions Yeshua (Jesus) mentioned Solomon, as he was the type/shadow of Himself as King of Kings. One must study this book carefully, as it can only pertain to those in the last days, of what our Lord is desiring in us, and how we must reflect His character and be a holy, spotless bride for Him.

The act of her "becoming the bride" is conditioned on her attaining these eight characteristics—symbolic not only of new beginnings and eternal life, but also of an invitation to dwell in the Holy of Holies with Him. As believers, we all have access to His holy presence, but it will be the bride that dwells in His presence.

Twice Speak

Behold, thou [art] fair, my love; behold, thou [art] fair...

—Song of Solomon 4:1

*T*he Hebrew word for "fair" is *Yaphah*, which means "beautiful," implying internal as well as external beauty, and refers to the Messiah. In this verse, Solomon is reaffirming His love for her growth and maturity.

Repetition is not only for emphasis, but is known as "twice speak" in scripture. Job 33:14-17 tells us:

For God speaketh once, yea twice, [yet man] perceiveth it not. In a dream, in a vision of the night, when deep sleep falleth upon men, in slumberings upon the bed; then he openeth the ears of men, and sealeth their instruction, that he may withdraw man [from his] purpose, and hide pride from man.

Yeshua did this several times in scripture. In Luke 10:41-42, He says, "And Jesus answered and said unto her, Martha, Martha, thou art careful and troubled about many things." In Matthew 23:37, He says, "O Jerusalem, Jerusalem, [thou] that killest the prophets, and stonest them which are sent unto thee, how often would I have gathered thy children together, even as a hen gathereth her chickens under [her] wings, and ye would not!" And Revelation 14:8 says, "And there followed another angel, saying, Babylon is fallen, is fallen, that great city, because she made all nations drink of the wine of the wrath of her fornication." Babylon has fallen and in the last days, it will fall again.

For example, in the Song of Solomon 8:5 the question is asked, "Who [is] this that cometh up from the wilderness?" This is referring to Mount Sinai and the forty years in the wilderness; but it is also addressed in the book of Revelation 12:6 and 12:14, when the bride is taken into the wilderness for protection and then is seen coming out victoriously.

Not only is the speaker directing his conversation to that particular person and situation, he is directing it toward the last-day saints. This is an indication that a particular event will play out twice. In this case, not only is Solomon speaking to his bride, the Shulamite, but as a picture of the Bridegroom he is speaking to the Bride of Messiah for last-day instructions on what we should look like. We must be careful to hear what the Spirit is saying.

Eyes as Innocent Doves

> Thou [hast] doves' eyes within thy locks...
> — Song of Solomon 4:1b

*T*he Shulamite is described as having innocent doves' eyes. The Hebrew word for "dove" is *Yownah*, which means "from the warmth of their mating." It is also the Hebrew name Jonah. Its root word, *Yayin*, means "effervesce, wine, and fermented."

Someone with "doves' eyes" is seen as beautiful, like a turtledove with singleness of purpose, devoted to her mate for a lifetime. As believers, our eyes should be of spiritual perception, veiled with a beauty and love set apart for the Messiah alone. A dove can only focus on one object at a time. They have no "peripheral vision;" thus, what He is saying to her is that her eyes are no longer "wandering" but they are "faithful." As she continues to behold Him, we find that she will increasingly become like Him. Just like the innocence of the dove.

The dove is also given as a sign. It was symbolic of the *Ruach Ha Kodesh*, or Holy Spirit, as mentioned in Matthew 3:16, when the Holy Spirit came upon the Lord as a dove and helped the Messiah complete His ministry while here on the earth.

In this verse we see the dove of the Spirit has not only come upon her but dwells within her. The Bridegroom can now see the Holy Spirit in her eyes and her life bears witness of it. The bride listens to the Spirit, does what the Spirit directs her to do, and welcomes His voice.

The dove was used as a "sign" to Noah. And, interestingly, "Jonah" means dove. In Luke 11:29, when Yeshua addressed the crowds seeking "a sign," he said no sign will be given to this generation except the sign of Jonah. Verse 30 says, "For as Jonah was a sign to the Ninevites, so shall also the Son of man will be to this generation." Jonah's time spent in the belly of the whale for three days and nights was a sign of Yeshua in the grave for three whole days and three whole nights.

Yeshua continues in verse 31 of Luke 11, "The queen of the south shall rise up in the judgment with the men of this generation, and condemn them: for she came from the utmost parts of the earth to hear the wisdom of Solomon; and, behold, a greater than Solomon [is] here."

The Lord's bride is not one who seeks understanding, but has her eyes fixed on the One *with* understanding.

Our prayer should be that "the eyes of your understanding being enlightened; that ye may know what is the hope of his calling, and what the riches of the glory of his inheritance in the saints," as it states in Ephesians 1:18.

And the bride's doves' eyes tell it all, don't they?

The Hebrew word for eyes is *Ahin*, which means "to put for several affections of the mind, the understanding, God's watchful providence, the Judgment, esteem, kind regard, desire good or bad, expectation, and compassion."

Continuing in Luke chapter 11, Yeshua says in verses 34 and 35, "The lamp of the body is the eye: therefore when thine eye is single, thy whole body also is full of light; but when [thine eye] is evil, thy body also [is] full of darkness.

Take heed therefore that the light which is in thee be not darkness."

Having a "single" eye refers to pure devotion while a "wandering" eye refers to a half-hearted or impure devotion.

Oddly, this Hebrew idiom that Yeshua uses could almost seem out of place here. When an eye is bad, it is considered stingy and when an eye is good, it is generous. Yet here, Yeshua is talking about the affections of the mind, desires good and bad—those kind and compassionate and in regards to judgment as described earlier. In this case, Yeshua warns us to take heed that the light which is in us is not darkness.

The Hebrew word for "darkness" is *Skotos*, and it comes from the root word *Ska*, "to cover." The darkness arises from error—truth hidden whether it be from ignorance, disobedience, willful blindness, or rebellion.

We certainly have a lot of error in the church today! He warned us to watch of this happening. Certainly, we should be kind and generous, not behaving greedy and lustful. For in doing so, we will fall into error and false doctrine, willful disobedience, blindness, and rebellion.

The Shulamite's eyes are full of light—she is not only generous, with kind regard, but she is void of error and ignorance. She is not near-sighted like Leah (and her descendants, which are not able to recognize the Messiah), but her eyes are bright and clear.

In Song of Solomon 4:1, the King exhorts the immature bride saying she has doves' eyes, hidden behind her "locks." Some translations say "veil"—hidden from the world.

The Hebrew word for "locks" is *Tsammah*, which is from an unused root meaning "to fasten on a veil." And the Hebrew word for "veil" is *Radiyd*, which is from the root word *Radad*, having the sense of "spreading; a veil." The veil is a sign of modesty, humility, and subjection.

The mention of the veil certainly supports the idea that this is in a public gathering. This veil covers the upper part of the face only, for Solomon is able to see clearly enough to describe in detail the facial features below her eyes. From beneath the veil, her eyes remind him of the pleasant softness and color of doves' eyes.

As the Bride of Christ, we see that her relationship with God is now "veiled" and thus her pure devotion is primarily for His pleasure. This pure devotion has also brought her to a place of security in her relationship with the King and therefore has no desire or need to show others her devotion or to be noticed by others.

The veil reveals much of her face—no longer hidden behind her veil as his betrothed, but pulled back, as it is a wedding, revealing to the world who she is. For now, we are hidden by a veil, for the world does not recognize who we are, but soon we will be with our Heavenly Bridegroom, ruling and reigning with Him and all will behold our beauty and splendor as His bride.

Hair as Goats

Thy hair [is] as a flock of goats, that appear
from mount Gilead.

— Song of Solomon 4:1c

One rabbi wrote, "Imagine the spreading out a flock of goats as they descend from a narrow mountain pathway into a valley. So do the strands of her hair, descending from her head, cover her shoulders and back."

We in the West may struggle in picturing this. Try to imagine this: hundreds of riders on Harley-Davidsons top the hill and spread across the desert—so do the strands of her hair. For some that would be a pretty sight!

The *Midrash* explains that this verse refers to the natural glossy black color of a goat like a strand or braid of hair. When the sun shone upon it, her hair glistened with a beautiful sheen. The picture of the flock of goats coming down from the mountainside in rows just before daybreak, formed white lines against the dark background in the dim light; this is like "when a woman has a luxuriant growth of hair she arranges it in white lines—showing the partings in between."

One writer suggests the church is being referred to here. The entire arrangement of the white rows is the elect in white garments, being arrayed in the dawn of the Messianic system, when the day dawns in the heart of the elect (2 Peter 1:19) who partake of the divine nature (2 Peter 1:4) and are called out of darkness into His marvelous light (2 Peter 2:9).

A woman's hair is considered her glory and biblically represents devotion or covenant. Thus, the Nazarene vow (covenant) caused the one taking it to not bring a razor upon his head.

The Hebrew word for "goats" is *Ez*, and its root *Azaz* means "to be stout" or "strong." The Hebrew word for "Gilead" is *Gilad*, and its root *Galed* means "heap of testimony." The King's declaration to the bride is that her covenant with Him is very strong (like a flock of goats) and stands as a testimony (like Gilead) to their growing relationship.

Here are some facts about Gilead:

1. The area around Gilead is a chain of mountains, east of Jordan, intersected by numerous valleys. The tribes of Reuben, Gad and half of Manasseh found a home there (Joshua 17:1).

2. Gilead was renowned for its rich pastures and countless flocks (Numbers 23:1, Micah 7:14). It lies in view of Jerusalem, which is significant because of the anticipation of the return of the Messiah and the end of this current age.

3. Gilead symbolized the place of peace for the elect. It was held in connection to the kings of Judah (Jeremiah 22:6). However, the kingship was removed because of their idolatry and given to those who became both kings and priests unto God (Revelation 5:10).

4. There was a balm in Gilead, yet the health of the people was not restored (Jeremiah 8:22) due to their idolatry (Jeremiah 8:19). The nations were also told to go up to Gilead (Hosea 12:11).

5. The destruction of the women of Gilead will be punished (Amos 1:13). This is the basis of the parable of the sheep and goats in Matthew 25.

6. The Messianic restoration will involve Benjamin taking Gilead (Obadiah 1:19); thus, the inheritance of Reuben, Gad, and half of Manasseh is elsewhere beyond the Jordan to the east.

Micah 7:14 shows that the people, which are the flock of the inheritance of the Messiah, will dwell alone in a forest in the midst of a garden land. They will feed in Bashan and Gilead as in the days of old. This period refers to the period after the destruction of the planet by the nations (Micah 7:8-17). Then, the restoration of the last days shall be as the Exodus and it will be to Gilead and Lebanon (Zechariah 10:10).

Some interesting events also occurred in Gilead:

1. The sons of Joseph were given the land of Gilead as their inheritance. The men who bought Joseph from his brothers (at the insistence of Judah) came from Gilead.

2. Jephthah resided in Gilead and caused a yearly event among the daughters of Zion to mourn his daughter's loss.

3. King Ahab lost his life in Gilead, and the false prophets loathed it.

4. Ramoth, in Gilead, was a city of refuge, among ten other cities. There are many references which include Gilead as a boundary.

5. David discovered "mighty men" coming from Gilead.

6. Moses viewed the promised land from Gilead.

7. Jacob built an altar and made a covenant in Gilead.

8. Gilead's balm is the desire of those who want to be healed, with its abundance of forests and rich pastures.

Gilead stands as a reminder of the power of the Lord to carry out His will through men of covenant. Jeremiah describes a time in the future when the people of God will have ultimate victory. Jeremiah 50:19-20 says:

And I will bring Israel (home) again to his habitation, and he shall feed (on the most fertile districts both west and east) on Carmel and Bashan, and his soul shall be satisfied upon mount Ephraim and Gilead. In those days, and in that time, saith the LORD, the iniquity of Israel shall be sought for, and [there shall be] none; and the sins of Judah, and they shall not be found; for I will pardon them whom I reserve (the remnant, who come forth after the long tribulation).

Solomon saw Gilead as a place of promise as did Jeremiah. The bride's eyes are focused on Yeshua, her promise, set between the victorious frame of her hair, which is her covenant with Him that is strong and stands as a testimony to the promise like Gilead.

Teeth like Sheep

> Thy teeth [are] like a flock [of sheep that are even] shorn, which came up from the washing; whereof every one bear twins, and none [is] barren among them.
>
> — Song of Solomon 4:2

*T*eeth represent the way we "break down" or rightly divide the Word of God. But Solomon's choice to say "flock" instead of one sheep is significant. The bride is complete—lacking nothing.

The Hebrew word for "teeth" is *Shen*, which means "tooth," as "sharp." It comes from the root word *Shanan*, which means "to point, to pierce, prick, sharpen, teach diligently, and whet." She no longer has the tendency to focus on only one biblical truth or doctrine, but rather has a balanced diet of the whole word of God as food for the soul.

The Hebrew word "shorn" is *Qatsab*, which means "to clip" or "chop." The flock of sheep described here are even shorn. No more fluff here! These are lean, mean, chomping machines. Remember, the fleece is where the burrs and dirt gets stuck.

Here the Shulamite is described as digging into God's word during her personal study time, no longer being contaminated by the opinions, ideas, and traditions of men.

What she receives from man's teaching is first "washed" before it is "divided." She now has the ability to discern that which is of the flesh from that which is of the spirit, separating that which is "good" from that which is "evil" (Hebrews 4:12, 5:14) as we are instructed to do. Hebrews 5:14 says, "But strong meat belongeth to them that are of full age, [even] those who by reason of use have their senses exercised to discern both good and evil."

Second, we read that the sheep that are shorn "came up from the washing." This washing is symbolic of a *Mikvah*. The sheep going down into the water dusty and dirty come up clean—a great word picture of baptism.

In Judaism, the *Mikvah* is described as returning to the womb and coming up being "reborn," or born again.

Now, the bride's mind is renewed, by the washing and cleansing of the water of the Word. Ephesians 5:26 says, "That he might sanctify and cleanse it with the washing of the water by the word."

Third, we read that "every one bear twins." This refers to the ability of the bride to recognize, counter, and balance truths. We are to know "the mercy and judgment" of God, we are to "suffer before we reign," and many like-balanced truths. The bride no longer swings like a pendulum with extreme doctrine.

Fourth, we read that "none [is] barren among them." This refers to the Word of God taking on life in her. No longer is it simply "head knowledge" but now it brings about change. None is barren—meaning there is fruit in her life and those around her.

The term "barren" speaks of being unable to bear children. Isaiah 54 declares that the days of barrenness are gone. The bride's words are fruit-filled and issue life. Isaiah 54:1-5 says:

> Sing, O barren, thou [that] didst not bear;
> break forth into singing, and cry aloud, thou
> [that] didst not travail with child: for more [are]

the children of the desolate than the children of the married wife, saith the LORD. Enlarge the place of thy tent, and let them stretch forth the curtains of thine habitations: spare not, lengthen thy cords, and strengthen thy stakes; for thou shalt break forth on the right hand and on the left; and thy seed shall inherit the Gentiles, and make the desolate cities to be inhabited. Fear not; for thou shalt not be ashamed: neither be thou confounded; for thou shalt not be put to shame: for thou shalt forget the shame of thy youth, and shalt not remember the reproach of thy widowhood any more. For thy Maker [is] thine husband; the LORD of hosts [is] his name; and thy Redeemer the Holy One of Israel; The God of the whole earth shall he be called.

Finally, the teeth are compared to the whiteness of newly-washed wool, the color of snow. Many of us probably have bought some of those toothpaste-brand "Complete Strips" wanting to get that sparkle back in our smile—but here's how to on what the LORD really desires!

Isaiah 1:18 says, "Come now, and let us reason together, saith the LORD: though your sins be as scarlet, they shall be as white as snow; though they be red like crimson, they shall be as wool." And Revelation 19:13-14 says:

> And he [was] clothed with a vesture dipped in blood: and his name is called The Word of God. And the armies [which were] in heaven followed him upon white horses, clothed in fine linen, white and clean. (That is His bride!)

The teeth are all alike like twins, as the elect that stand before the throne of God in washed robes in the blood of the Lamb. We all must be spiritually prepared to stand before the throne.

Lips like Scarlet Thread

Thy lips [are] like a thread of scarlet...

— Song of Solomon 4:3a

*T*he Hebrew word for "lips" is *Saphah*, which comes from the root *Sepheth*, meaning "the lip as a natural boundary, language, speech, talk, and vain words."

Lips speak of our speech and refer to what we say. Her lips are like a thread of scarlet. Good news for those who have thin lips! So much for the Hollywood ideal of thick, voluptuous lips!

The Hebrew word for "thread" is *Khoot*, which means "to sew" or "a string." If we go by analogy, her lips are "sewn together," thus her words are few. She no longer speaks a multitude of vain or empty words.

A thread is something we would sew with. It speaks of something that ties things together. Her words are directed and pointed, binding together the multitude of truths that she has learned. Her words mend and bind, bringing healing to wounds caused by the lies of the enemy.

As a narrow strand of color, the red hue of scarlet speaks of redemption. She no longer speaks out of bitterness or opinion. When she speaks, it has a meaningful and redemptive quality to it.

The mention of scarlet here immediately brings to mind Rahab and the scarlet cord she extended for the spies at the wall of Jericho. In this verse, we are reminded of the salvation extended to the Gentiles through the scarlet blood of Christ, our Passover sacrifice.

The use of the term "scarlet thread" has powerful significance for those things that have holy use, as well as how the scarlet thread neatly ties the first and renewed covenant together as mentioned in Hebrews 9:19-22:

> For when Moses had spoken every precept to all the people according to the law, he took the blood of calves and of goats, with water, and scarlet wool, and hyssop, and sprinkled

both the book, and all the people, saying, This
is the blood of the testament (covenant) which
God hath enjoined unto you. Moreover he
sprinkled with blood both the tabernacle, and
all the vessels of the ministry. And almost all
things are by the law purged with blood; and
without shedding of blood is no remission.

These are similar words that Yeshua said after the
Passover *Seder* in Matthew 26:27-28: "Drink ye all of it; for
this is my blood of the new testament (covenant), which is
shed for many for the remission of sins."

Every place where the Hebrew word *Shani* (scarlet)
has been used as it is used in the Song has reference to holy
use in worship and ceremony. There are two references in
scripture that are outside these boundaries.

Genesis 38 pictures a scarlet thread in the birth of
the last-born twins of Judah. One of the twins threw forth
his hand, and the midwife bound it with a scarlet thread,
declaring he was the first born. That twin brought back his
hand into the womb, and his brother was born first. If we
perceive the womb as a grave, we see the death and resurrec-
tion and what it means to be born again. Yeshua is the first

born from the grave, yet we are the ones who will be characterized as the ones with the "scarlet thread."

The other use of the word *Shani* outside ceremonial reference is found in 2 Samuel 1:25. David instructed the daughters of Israel to weep for Saul's death. He declares that Saul "clothed you in scarlet, with [other] delights." Yeshua clothes His bride in His blood and bought redemption, and at His right are pleasures for evermore.

Beautiful Speech

Thy speech is comely...

— Song of Solomon 4:3b

*T*he Hebrew word for "speech" is *Midbar*, and it comes from the root word *Dabar*, having the sense of "driving, a pasture, a desert;" also "speech" including its organs. The Hebrew word *Dabar* means "to arrange," but used figuratively concerning words to speak.

The Hebrew word for "mouth" is *Peh*, and means "thy speech" or "the instruments of thy speech." The sense of her speech being comely or lovely—meaning "perfect"— is how He originally created her. In fact, this was the condition of Satan before the fall; his instruments were perfect until iniquity was found in him (Ezekiel 28:13-15).

Does Yeshua expect His bride to be perfect? Yes, He does! Yeshua also said it was not what goes into the body that defiles the man, but what comes out of his mouth. Matthew 15:11 says, "Not that which goeth into the mouth defileth a man; but that which cometh out of the mouth, this defileth a man."

The King refers to her speech as "comely" because no deceit or bitterness comes out of her mouth. She speaks the pure Word of God, undefiled by the flesh. 1 Peter 3:10 says, "For he that will love life, and see good days, let him refrain his tongue from evil, and his lips that they speak no guile."

Lips serve to guard the tongue—which is a sword and weapon. Isaiah 54:17 says, "No weapon that is formed against thee shall prosper; and every tongue [that] shall rise against thee in judgment thou shalt condemn." "Death and life [are] in the power of the tongue" as it warns in Proverbs 18:21.

Nearly every act of belief begins with a confession, whether it is an act of believing for mountains to be moved or the first confession of a repentant sinner. As his bride, we are to call into existence things that are not, through "comely speech." Believers are to say what the Word of God says regarding their situation. Mark 11:23 says:

> For verily I say unto you, That whosoever shall say unto this mountain, Be thou removed, and be thou cast into the sea; and shall not doubt in his heart, but shall believe that those things which he saith shall come to pass; he shall have whatsoever he saith.

It's not just about looking at a picture of a Cadillac on your mirror and telling yourself you are going to get it, or deserve it, because you are a saint. It is much more than that. Here her tongue speaks faith-filled promises. Her words pronounce victory before the battle.

James taught us that our tongues are like a fire that no man can tame. In Judaism, this evil communication is called *Loshon Hora*, which literally means "evil talk." It is defined as information which is either derogatory or potentially harmful to another individual.

Rechilus is the second form of *Loshon Hora*, and means "peddling" or "one who engages in carrying a tale."

The third form is *Motzi Shem Ra*, which means "slander."

Onaas devarim, the fourth form of *Loshon Hora*, is defined as "causing pain with words." The Torah looks upon emotional pain as a real wound, as opposed to the "words can't hurt me" childhood lie. Other types of speech a believer must avoid are words of anger, arrogance, deceit, lying, and false flattery.

Loshon Hora is a weapon manufactured solely from words, yet the Torah considers the harm it creates to be massive. The Jews believe that *Loshon Hora* drives a wedge between a believer and Yahweh, and that it can even deprive him of Divine assistance in a time of need.

This is speech that does not proceed from the mouth of the Beloved's bride. Her speech is life-filled concerning the kingdom of God.

Temples like Pomegranate

Thy temples [are] like a piece of a pomegranate
within thy locks.

— Song of Solomon 4:3b

*T*he slight indentation of the temples is quite
distinct from beneath the veil and Solomon finds
it yet another feature to praise. The Hebrew
word *Raqqah* means "temple thinness or temple, upper cheek
region," and refers to the seat of intelligence.

The temple speaks of our mind or our seat of intel-
lect. Where our mind is fixed, the rest of our body goes. It
is in the "temporal region" of our brain that our motor
functions are controlled; thus the temples speak of self-
control.

Solomon uses the pomegranate theme for her temples to show fertility of the mind, a mind where good seed is

planted and a harvest is sure. Her thoughts are on what is pure, lovely, and of good report. She is the true bride, with the mental state that matches the King's. It is here the Holy Spirit finds a welcome depository for "things that are to come." Here the words of Yeshua are quickly brought to mind. She has the mind of Christ.

The Hebrew word for "pomegranate" is *Ramam*, which means "to rise up" or "to be mounted up." They were the principal ornaments of the stately columns of Solomon's temple.

The pomegranate fruit, in relation to her temples, signifies that it is now the "fruit of the Spirit" that controls her life (mounts or raises us up or above) rather than the lust of the flesh. The phrase "within thy locks" shows that she bears spiritual fruit that is veiled and hidden from the world for only the Lord to behold.

Many interpreters believe the reference to pomegranates is a symbol of fertility. On a holy theme, greater significance might point to the use of the pomegranate as it relates to the skirt of the high priest. At the bottom of the high priest's robe, pomegranates were interspersed with bells. With every step, the ringing of bells with the symbol for "fertility of life" bore witness to sight and sound declaring life. Life and abundance characterizes the Savior's bride.

Rashi explains that the temples, as a pomegranate split open behind the veil, refers to a glowing complexion and the roundness of the cheeks.

One author suggests this reference is to the elect. The "splitting open" perhaps refers to the curtain. The elect now can go in behind the veil since it was torn in two by the sacrifice of the Messiah. Symbolizing the ruddy color, the play on words places the bride at the inner sanctuary.

Neck like the Tower of David

Thy neck [is] like the tower of David built for
an armory, whereon there hang a thousand
bucklers, all shields of mighty men.

— Song of Solomon 4:4

*T*he neck speaks of the will of man. The Israelites
were referred to as a "stiff-necked" people; thus
their will would not be broken and submitted to
God. This is in sharp contrast to being "broken" and
"contrite," which speaks of our will being broken and
submitted to the Father.

First, the King exhorts "thy neck [is] like the tower
of David." This speaks of, by analogy, being a "man after
God's own heart." Being a man after God's own heart is a
man completely submitted to His Lordship. It also speaks of
strength. The bride's will is submitted, but it is strong as an
"anchor" and support to others of the faith.

The shield speaks of faith (as in the shield of faith) for the bride. Ephesians 6:13-18 says:

> Wherefore take unto you the whole armor of God, that ye may be able to withstand in the evil day, and having done all, to stand. Stand therefore, having your loins girt about with truth, and having on the breastplate of righteousness; and your feet shod with the preparation of the gospel of peace; above all, taking the shield of faith, wherewith ye shall be able to quench all the fiery darts of the wicked. And take the helmet of salvation, and the sword of the Spirit, which is the word of God: praying always with all prayer and supplication in the Spirit, and watching thereunto with all perseverance and supplication for all saints.

The next phrase, "built for an armory, whereon there hang a thousand bucklers, all shields of mighty men," tells us that the Lord will strengthen us to "do the will of the Father." We will become a pillar in His household and will raise up many "mighty men."

Armories speak of armies and those going to battle. War is a matter of pitting two irreconcilable wills against one another, and He is certainly preparing His bride for battle. Our will can be strong in a positive sense of submission and thus be "flexible," or it can be strong in rebellion and thus be referred to as being "stiff-necked."

Yeshua sees His maturing bride as not being stiff-necked, but rather submitting her will to Him. She no longer stands in open rebellion to the King but chooses to respond to His outpouring of love by humbling herself before Him. In this, we see the wisdom of God in how He chooses to break the will of man. He chooses to make us broken through love and affection.

How lovely is her neck which is not bowed in shame or defeat. It is a neck "like the tower of David," which was built for a fortress and an arsenal for weapons of battle.

Straight and erect, not deranged or depressed—she stands for a world to admire her beauty. A thousand shields of faith depict a state of preparedness. The bride is not a weak child, unable to defend herself and unprepared. According to one source, the shields were used as ornaments, as Ezekiel 27:11 says: "They hanged their shields upon thy walls round about; they have made thy beauty perfect." However, we know we must be prepared physically as well as spiritually for what lies ahead in the last days.

Breasts like Young Roes

Thy two breasts [are] like two young roes that
are twins, which feed among the lilies.

— Song of Solomon 4:5

*B*reasts speak of our ability to nourish others. We
see in this the expression "two young roes that
are twins" that twins speak of balanced truth.
The maturing bride now has the ability to present the whole
council of God perfectly balanced. "Young" speaks of
"fresh revelation;" thus what is being fed has timing and
relevance to it. Just like daily manna from heaven, it is truth
for today and for those in the last days, who are part of the
remnant bride.

The Hebrew word for "roe" is *Tsebiy*, and means
"splendor" or "prominence." Those who nourish the body
will be exalted, but not as man sees it. Our honor is not with

man, and those who are part of the bride remain hidden from the world's eyes.

The King goes on to say "which feed among the lilies." Lilies are common, but were used as ornaments in the Temple! Song of Solomon 2:1-2 says, "I [am] the rose of Sharon, [and] the lily of the valleys. As the lily among thorns, so [is] my love among the daughters."

The lily of the valley was in great multitude; thus the expression "which feed among the lilies" refers to the bride walking in the midst of the common, ordinary people (and she is common and ordinary), revealing God's truth as food for the multitude.

Feeding amongst the lilies is in very sharp contrast to "standing above, over others." Again, the bride walks veiled (hidden) amongst humanity in the flesh as Yeshua did, yet ministers to people what they need, when they need it.

The Messiah directly refers to this concept in Matthew 6:28-29:

> Consider the lilies of the field, how they
> grow; they toil not, neither do they spin: and yet

Breasts like Young Roes

I say unto you, that even Solomon in all his glory was not arrayed like one of these.

The bride is pictured as a woman, and is in fact the second Eve. Her breasts are the place of nurture where the sincere milk of the word is obtained. She cuddles new believers and helps them grow.

No Spot in Thee

Until the day break, and the shadows flee away,
I will get me to the mountain of myrrh, and to
the hill of frankincense. Thou [art] all fair, my
love; [there is] no spot in thee.

> — Song of Solomon 4:6-7

One translation says, "Until the cool of the day..."
The cool of the day symbolizes the joy of meeting
His beloved as He did in the garden with Adam at
the end of the day. This refers to His Millennial reign.

Myrrh and frankincense were both gifts given by the
Magi at Yeshua's birth, as seen in Matthew 2:11:

And when they were come into the house,
they saw the young child with Mary his mother,
and fell down, and worshipped him: and when
they had opened their treasures, they presented

unto him gifts; gold, and frankincense, and myrrh.

Myrrh is symbolic of Yeshua as a suffering servant—it was used at His burial. Frankincense is symbolic of Yeshua as our High Priest—it was burnt on the altar, while some was set aside on the showbread, as it was holiest to Him.

The reference to having "no spot" is a priestly term—without spot or wrinkle. Ephesians 5:26-27 says:

> That he might sanctify and cleanse it with the washing of water by the word, that he might present it to himself a glorious church, not having spot, or wrinkle, or any such thing; but that it should be holy and without blemish.

Oh, what a time we have to look forward to for those who desire to become this picture-perfect bride! Yes, the bride stands as a figure of beauty, growing more beautiful each day, until there shall be none to compare to her!

Rebecca at the Well Foundation is a non-profit Judeo-Christian organization devoted to inspiring true believers to prepare for the return of the Messiah. By informing true believers the way to walk in the beauty of holiness, it motivates members of the body to be clothed with righteous acts and deeds as the Bride of Christ.

In an effort to bridge the gap between Judaism and Christianity, Rebecca at the Well Foundation provides workshops and seminars about the Hebraic roots of our faith that binds us together as one. All believers can celebrate His return as they learn how to make themselves ready as a pure and holy bride.

Rebecca Park Totilo, founder and president of the Rebecca at the Well Foundation, is currently touring the country, preparing the bride for her Heavenly Bridegroom. She is available to speak at conferences, seminars and retreats. Please contact her at (727) 688-2115 for more information, or if you would like to have her come and share with your group or congregation.

Visit our website at:
www.RebeccaAtTheWell.org or www.RebeccaTotilo.com

For e-mail correspondence, please write:
becca@RebeccaAtTheWell.org

For snail mail correspondence:
Rebecca at the Well Foundation
P.O. Box 60044
St. Petersburg, FL 33784

To order additional copies of

A Portrait of the Bride: The Shulamite

Have your credit card ready and call:
1 – 727 – 688 – 2115

or please visit our website at
www.rebeccaatthewell.org

Other Book & CD Sets:
The Dance of the Shulamite
A Portrait of the Bride: Rebekah
Draw Me to the Secret Place Series
The Fragrance of the Bride
Who Is the Bride?

Notes

Notes

Notes

Notes

Notes

Notes

www.ingramcontent.com/pod-product-compliance
Lightning Source LLC
Chambersburg PA
CBHW071022040426
42443CB00007B/904